MICHIGAN SOLDIERS
in the
CIVIL WAR

· · · · · · ·

By
Frederick D. Williams

A *Michigan History Magazine* Heritage Publication

Michigan Historical Center
Michigan Department of State
Lansing, Michigan
1998

Other heritage publications from
Michigan History Magazine:

Father Marquette's Journal
When the Railroad Was King
Subject Guide to Michigan History Magazine, *1978-1994*
No Tears In Heaven
Michigan and the Civil War: An Anthology

Visit *Michigan History Magazine* and its growing family of
heritage publications on the World Wide Web:
www.sos.state.mi.us/history/mag/mag.html

Michigan Soldiers in the Civil War
Fourth Edition
ISBN 0-935719-57-1
© 1998 Michigan Historical Center, Michigan Department of State

Printed on recycled paper.
This product was not printed at Michigan taxpayer expense.
MH-140 (rev. 11/98)

Michigan Department of State
Candice S. Miller, Secretary of State

Contents

• • • • • • •

Introduction

· · · · · · ·

y earliest introduction to Fred Williams occurred during the early 1960s. As a middle schooler, I wrote to history agencies all across the nation requesting any free literature they had on their state's involvement in the Civil War. Most states sent me something. But I was most impressed with the "blue books" from the Michigan Civil War Centennial Observance Commission. In fact, I wrote the Michigan commission so often that I received a letter politely telling me to go away.

Professor Frederick Williams of Michigan State University was one of the three members of the commission's publications committee. It is fortunate for Michigan that he was. Today, those 25 blue-covered books remain a lasting tribute to Michigan's role in the nation's greatest and most tragic conflict.

Besides directing the commission's publications efforts, Professor Williams authored *Michigan Soldiers in the Civil War*. His manuscript first appeared in *Michigan History Magazine* before being published as a book. That was in the 1960s. After several reprintings and two subsequent editions, *Michigan Soldiers* remains our most popular publication. It is a great introduction to the role of the thousands of Michiganians who, as Professor Williams points out in our special 1998 Civil War issue, "gave so much for freedom and democracy." This fourth edition has been expanded to include a new design, more photographs and an updated reading list.

This latest edition also affords me an opportunity to thank Fred for his input in my career as a historian. During the late 1970s I spent much of my graduate career at MSU taking all his courses and working as his teaching assistant. Ultimately, Fred directed my doctoral dissertation. Today, as I edit *Michigan History Magazine* and teach history courses at MSU, including a class on the Civil War, I realize how fortunate I am to have been his student. He instilled in me a greater understanding of American history, and I am reminded of the importance he placed on teaching it every time I step behind the lectern.

Roger L. Rosentreter
December 1998

Immortalized by photographer Mathew Brady, this soldier of Company C, Fourth Michigan Infantry, sports a Zouave cap and—like many Michiganians who joined the service in 1861—a determined countenance.

The Ascendancy
of Confederate Arms

• • • • • • •

The Blow at Last Fallen. War! War! War! The Confederate Batteries Open on Sumter Yesterday Morning." This blazing headline carried by the *Detroit Free Press* on April 13, 1861, announced the end of angry sectional conflict and the beginning of a new and more trying era. "The war is inaugurated," declared one of Michigan's leading citizens, "and there should be no flinching now."

On April 15, the day after Fort Sumter fell, President Abraham Lincoln issued a proclamation calling for 75,000 militia to put down an insurrection by combinations "too powerful to be suppressed by the ordinary course of judicial proceedings." Michigan was asked to furnish one regiment of infantry, and her response was swift and complete. But the patriotic outburst that swept the nation after Sumter soon subsided and subsequent calls for volunteers left much to be desired. Thus it became necessary for the Union to undertake its initial experiment in compulsory military service. The draft was extremely unpopular, even with the soldiers who derisively referred to the men in civilian life as the Home Guard. One rub was, as a Michigan infantryman asserted, that the draft made one "ashamed of his countrymen." Then, too, there was considerable bitterness over the provision that enabled a draftee to avoid service by hiring a substitute or by paying a sum of $300. This was one reason why many called the Civil War "a rich man's war and a poor man's fight."

During the first year of the conflict 21 Michigan regiments were organized; before the fighting stopped more Michigan men had donned the blue than Lincoln had called for in his April proclamation. Besides raising a total of 45 regiments—31 infantry, 11 cavalry and one each of engineers and mechanics, artillery and sharpshooters—Michigan contributed soldiers to over 50 other military units and sent nearly 600 men

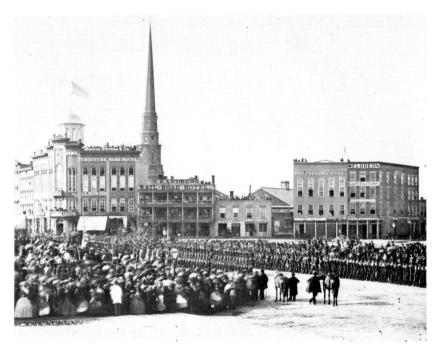

In May 1861, when the First Michigan Infantry (above, in Detroit) arrived in Washington DC , President Lincoln was credited with exclaiming, "Thank God for Michigan!"

to serve in the Union navy. The procedure for raising troops was inefficient, expensive and fraught with politics. Although calls for men came from the federal government, most of the recruiting was done by the states and in some cases by individuals. When the president called for troops, Michigan, along with the other loyal states, was assigned a quota. If new regiments were to be created, the governor authorized a specific number, appointed the regimental officers and gave them responsibility for raising and organizing their own units. On occasion the federal government, with the approval of the governor, commissioned men with influence or military experience to raise one or more regiments. The state legislatures appropriated large sums of money to clothe and equip the soldiers, and patriotic citizens made contributions for this same purpose. The federal, state and local governments, private organizations and individuals encouraged voluntary enlistments by offering a sum of money, a bounty, to men who agreed to enter the service.

Thousands of soldiers who enlisted for three years were eligible to go home either in 1864 or 1865; but patriotism and the promise of bounties and furloughs induced most of these men to reenlist. The Michigan regiments were mustered into the service in 21 different towns and cities, and, when time permitted, were given preliminary training in one of the several camps that sprang up as the need arose. The ranks were filled with men from across the state, from all walks of life. The names of nearly 89,000 whites, 1,660 African Americans and 145 Native Americans appear on the state's Civil War roster. Indeed, during the war years more than half of the Michigan men of military age served in the armed forces of the United States.

Even a few Michigan women managed to enter the service as men. The state's most famous female soldier was Sarah Emma Edmonds, who enlisted in 1861 as Franklin Thompson, concealing her gender and identity for two years. During her service in the Second Michigan she participated in several campaigns. As a spy for the Union she had some frightening experiences, narrowly escaping with her life on a number of occasions. Although she used several disguises for her secret operations, it seems that her best cover-up was that of a woman.

This June 1861 *New York Illustrated News* woodcut depicts the Third Michigan Infantry parading down Detroit's Jefferson Avenue on its way to Washington DC.

Kinchen Artis joined the First Michigan Colored Infantry in 1863. His is one of the few existing images of members of the state's only African American regiment. Reassigned as the 102nd U.S. Colored Troops, this unit left Detroit in March 1864. It saw service in South Carolina, Georgia and Florida before returning home to Michigan in October 1865.

Michigan's First Colored Infantry was mustered into service in February 1864. Known later as the 102nd Regiment United States Colored Troops, it campaigned in South Carolina and Florida, destroying Confederate supply lines. Sometimes under a blazing Southern sun, soldiers of the 102nd trampled through reptile-infested swamps and fought off enemy troops in order to complete their missions. Despite numerous hardships they wrecked many miles of Southern railroads and contributed materially to the Union victory.

The first Michigan regiments to leave for combat joined General Irvin McDowell's army in and around Washington in spring 1861. In mid-July, about 25 miles south, near Manassas, Virginia, General Pierre Gustave Toutant Beauregard had a Confederate force in good position along the south bank of a lazy stream called Bull Run. Satisfied that the Union army was capable of whipping the enemy, with cries of "On to Richmond" ringing in his ears, Lincoln ordered an attack.

McDowell's original plan was to strike the Confederate right flank near Blackburn's Ford. On July 18, 1861, he probed to ascertain the enemy's strength at that position. An in-depth reconnaissance was conducted by General Israel B. Richardson, whose brigade included the Second and Third Michigan Infantries. As the troops approached the ford, enemy muskets cracked. A sharp engagement ensued. Mounting resistance indicated unexpected Confederate strength and Richardson withdrew. The intelligence from this reconnaissance caused McDowell to abandon his original plan in favor of an assault against the enemy left.

On July 21, a sweltering Sunday, the Union army struck. In the early fighting the Confederates lost one position after another. For a while it seemed nothing could save them from disaster. But as the day wore on, their resistance stiffened. Shortly after noon the First Michigan Infantry approached the Henry House, where the most savage fighting of the battle took place. With Colonel Orlando B. Willcox barking out orders, the Michigan men charged the enemy troops that had just captured a Union battery. A murderous volley of shot and shell drove them back. From high ground behind the Confederate line, enemy artillery sprayed the approach to the captured guns. In a strip of woods, well within musket range, three gray-clad brigades poured bullets into the advancing ranks. Four assaults against this strong position gained nothing but

After the war, Captain William H. Withington (left) of the First Michigan Infantry received the Medal of Honor for administering aid and comfort to his wounded commander, Colonel Orlando Willcox (right), at the Battle of Bull Run in July 1861.

a growing list of casualties. Willcox was wounded and taken prisoner. About mid-afternoon the Union offensive sputtered to a halt. The Southerners soon seized the initiative and mounted an attack that threw the Federals into full retreat. When darkness came, the Confederates held the field. All through the night the defeated Union army fell back to the defenses around Washington. The withdrawal was covered by Richardson's brigade, with the Second and Third Michigan Infantries bringing up the rear. The next day a soldier in the Second wrote in his diary:

> *It was a terrible sight to see the wagons coming in last night loaded with dead, cut, torn and mangled in every possible manner and the wounded running or hobbling along with arms & legs dangling or hanging by shreds or crawling on the ground dragging their limbs slowly after them crushed, broken, or torn off entirely.*

Immediately after the Union defeat, which portended a long, hard struggle, Lincoln put General George McClellan in charge of the Union armies. McClellan devoted the next eight months to building and training the eastern Army of the Potomac. In March 1862 he launched a campaign on the peninsula between the York and James Rivers in Virginia. After landing about 112,000 men on the tip of the peninsula, he started toward Richmond—slowly and cautiously.

At Williamsburg the retreating Confederates turned on the Federals and checked their advance. In severe fighting, much of it at close quarters, the Second, Third and Fifth Michigan Infantries distinguished themselves. Colonel Henry D. Terry of Detroit, commander of the Fifth, reported that his men advanced in line of battle, holding their fire until they got in close. Then, in a hail of bullets, they charged. The enemy quickly retired to rifle pits, opening "a brisk fire with severe effect." Another charge was ordered, Terry recounted, "and our men marched up on double-quick and leaped into the rifle-pits, carried the position and retained it." A reporter claimed that the trenches in front of the Fifth were strewn with the bodies of 63 dead rebels, "every one of them

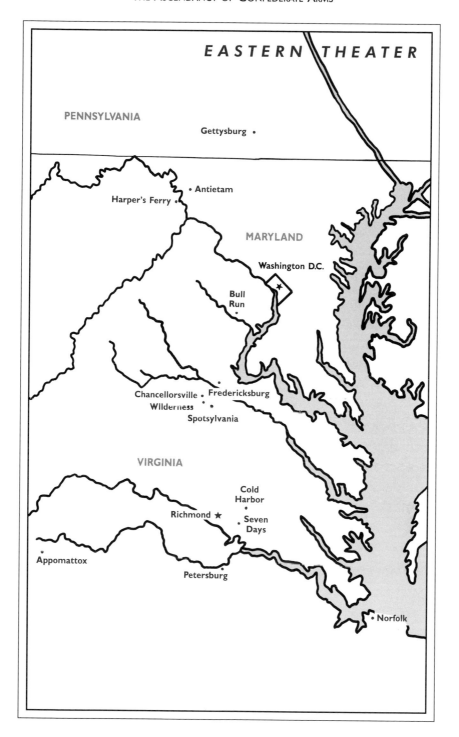

Colonel Dwight A. Woodbury of Adrian was killed while rallying the Fourth Michigan Infantry at Malvern Hill on July 1, 1862.

killed by the bayonet." The Michigan regiment also bled. Of the 500 men it sent into the fight, 34 were killed and 119 wounded.

The day after Williamsburg the Confederates resumed their retreat. By the end of May they faced the Union army a few miles from Richmond. The fighting in front of the city began at Fair Oaks and wound up with a series of brutal battles known as the Seven Days (June 25-July 1, 1862). Michigan soldiers fought in most of these struggles, including Malvern Hill, one of the most terrible battles of the war. An officer in the Second Michigan Infantry reported that his regiment marched to the right and front of the line and for three hours held an exposed position while enemy guns and muskets pounded the men. A doctor in the Fourth Michigan Infantry wrote that towards evening, soldiers in another regiment of his brigade charged the advancing rebels "half way across the field [but] the fire was so severe they were compelled to break and fall back in great confusion, passing the Fourth Michigan regiment, who were lying on their faces to escape the fire of the enemy." At that point, the doctor continued, Colonel Dwight A. Woodbury of Adrian, commander of the Fourth,

attempted to rally the retreating regiment, shouting to them, with his cap in one hand and his sword in the other, telling them to stand their ground, that they and the Fourth could check the enemy. At this moment he was pierced in the forehead by a musket ball. He threw up his arms and fell back dead.

Following a year of brutal campaigning, the Sixteenth Michigan Infantry settled into winter quarters near Fredericksburg, Virginia, during early 1863.

Shortly after Malvern Hill, Lincoln ordered McClellan to withdraw from the peninsula. From the Union point of view, the campaign seemed a complete failure. Richmond was still in rebel hands and the Confederate Army of Northern Virginia, now under General Robert E. Lee, remained a formidable fighting machine. In fact, it was about to open an offensive that shook the Union.

The withdrawal of McClellan's army from the peninsula gave Lee an opportunity for a bold strike against General John Pope, who had just been given command of a Union force in northern Virginia. If Lee moved quickly he might be able to destroy Pope before McClellan could join him. With General Thomas Jonathan "Stonewall" Jackson in the lead, the Confederates headed north. After whipping a Federal force at Cedar Mountain, Jackson executed a spectacular flanking movement that put him near Manassas, squarely on the rear of Pope's army. As Lee came up with the rest of his divisions, the fight got under way.

The Second Battle of Bull Run in late August 1862 was a costly, humiliating defeat of badly out-generaled Federal troops. The soldiers in the ranks, which included eight Michigan regiments, gave all that could be expected. In the corps of General Fitz-John Porter was the First Michigan Infantry, whose chaplain wrote that the regiment was ordered to charge and capture an enemy battery that was shattering

Union columns from a commanding position overlooking the front. So sure were the officers of the death that awaited them that "they shook hands with each other in farewell." As the Michigan soldiers advanced, the enemy opened fire with several hitherto concealed guns. Caught in a "cross-fire from five batteries at short range, throwing grape and canister, and . . . a flank fire of infantry," the men, continued the chaplain, "fell like grain in harvest." About half of the 250 officers and men were casualties. Eight officers fell in the early fighting. Among them was the regimental commander, Colonel Horace S. Roberts. Hit in the chest by a minié ball, Roberts moaned, "I am killed." Ten minutes later he was dead.

After his victory in the Second Battle of Bull Run, Lee decided to invade the North. His purpose was to win Maryland over to the Confederacy, demoralize the Union and perhaps bring the war to an early end. In all of these hopes, he was disappointed, for the Army of the Potomac caught up with him at Sharpsburg, Maryland, a quiet little town on the west bank of Antietam Creek. There, on September 17, 1862—the bloodiest day of the war—the two armies mauled each other in what has been called a defeat for both sides. Yet from a diplomatic standpoint, Antietam was the most important battle of the war. It enabled Lincoln to turn the conflict into a crusade against slavery—a move that helped immeasurably in keeping England, whose people abhorred slavery, from intervening in the war on behalf of the Confederacy.

The woods and fields of Antietam witnessed awful sights that hot September day—a day on which 350 Michigan men were killed, wounded or missing. There was the cornfield where the tide of battle surged back and forth, as desperate, half-crazed men met head-on. They shot, stabbed and clubbed one another until the torn earth assumed a crimson hue and the 30-acre field could be crossed by walking on the bodies of the dead. On the edge of the cornfield stood the Dunker church, where charging Federal regiments were hit full blast by a Confederate division and sent scampering for safer ground to the rear. Two miles to the south stood a stone bridge, over which Federal troops double-quicked as Confederate guns and muskets smashed them from the heights overlooking the crossing. In the center of the battlefield stretched a sunken road,

An 1841 West Point graduate, Israel B. "Fighting Dick" Richardson of Pontiac went off to war as commander of the Second Michigan Infantry. He received his first star following the Battle of Bull Run and his second star after commanding a division during the Peninsula Campaign. In savage fighting at the Battle of Antietam, Richardson was mortally wounded. He died on November 3, 1862.

where bloody fighting developed when Yankee columns charged the enemy line. The Confederates held their fire until the attackers were but a few yards away. Then, "Fire," roared the commander, and blazing rifles poured a volley into the faces of the Federals.

Watching from a position nearby was one of the finest and bravest officers that Michigan sent into the war, General Israel B. Richardson of Pontiac. Having entered the service as commander of the Second Michigan Infantry, Richardson fought in the Peninsula Campaign and attracted considerable attention for his fine soldierly qualities and ability to lead. Less than three months before Antietam, he was promoted to the rank of major general and entered the battle commanding a division. As Richardson's men moved towards the sunken road, soon known as Bloody Lane, the Michigan general, sensing the gravity of the situation, ordered a battery to support his advance. While directing the artillery fire, he fell mortally wounded. At the eastern end of Bloody Lane there now stands a tower overlooking the Antietam battleground. A few feet from its base is the barrel of an upright Union gun, marking the spot where Richardson fell.

For three months after Antietam, no major battles were fought in the eastern theater. Lee, his invasion thwarted, withdrew his army into northern Virginia. McClellan seemed content to let him go. Several weeks passed, but still the Union commander showed no sign of opening a large-scale offensive against Lee. In the interim he did find time for a public criticism of the administration in Washington. By early November the president's patience reached the point of exhaustion. He dismissed McClellan, placing bewhiskered General Ambrose E. Burnside in command of the Army of the Potomac.

Burnside's tenure in that capacity lasted less than three months and is marked by one of the most colossal failures of the war. As the Union army advanced southward, Lee occupied the heights just west of Fredericksburg on the right bank of the Rappahannock River. Burnside's first great problem was crossing the stream. In front of the town an attempt was made to build a pontoon bridge. But Confederate sharpshooters, firing from brick houses, cellars and rifle pits, killed so many workmen that construction was halted until the enemy could be cleared from the opposite bank.

A tremendous artillery barrage failed to do the trick, so Burnside called for volunteers to cross the river and establish a bridgehead. Colonel Norman J. Hall, commanding a brigade that included the

Lieutenant Norman J. Hall of Monroe, who graduated from West Point in 1854, served with U.S. forces defending Fort Sumter in April 1861. In July 1862 he was promoted to colonel of the Seventh Michigan Infantry. Hall played a prominent role as a brigade commander at Fredericksburg and Gettysburg. He was discharged due to disability in 1864; he died three years later.

Seventh Michigan Infantry, offered to do the job. Major Thomas H. Hunt, who took charge of the Michigan regiment during the mission, described the assault, reporting that "at a given signal the men rushed to the boats, carried them to the water, jumped into them, and pushed

WESTERN THEATER

Perryville •

KENTUCKY

MISSOURI

Fort Henry • • Fort Donelson

ARKANSAS

TENNESSEE

Stones
• River

Lookout
Mountain-
Chattanooga • • Missionary Ridge

Shiloh •

Corinth •

Chickamauga •

MISSISSIPPI

•
Atlanta

ALABAMA

GEORGIA

LOUISIANA • Vicksburg

•
Andersonville

FLORIDA

GULF OF MEXICO

off gallantly out into the stream amidst a shower of bullets." When they reached the opposite shore, a rousing cheer went up from the Union side. Then up the riverbank and into the town they scurried. A war correspondent found it amusing to watch the "rebels pop up by the hundred, like so many rats, from every cellar rifle pit and stone wall, and scamper off up the streets of the town." The Seventh, along with two Massachusetts regiments, held the bridgehead while the Federals spanned the stream.

On December 13, two days after the bridges spanning the Rappahannock River were completed, Burnside attacked the impregnable position held by Lee's army. In one sector of the Confederate line, troops under General James Longstreet fought from a sunken road behind a stone wall, in front of which stretched an open plain that descended toward the Union line. Against this strong position Burnside hurled regiments, brigades and divisions in a day-long frontal attack. Just before sundown the First Division of the Fifth Corps was ordered to advance and seize a hill about 500 yards in front of the enemy. In the division were three of the eleven Michigan infantry regiments at Fredericksburg: the First, Fourth and Sixteenth. Colonel Thomas B. W. Stockton of the Sixteenth led a brigade in this twilight attack, about which he wrote:

My whole line went briskly forward and when we had reached an intervening crest, about half way, we became entirely exposed to view, the rebels opened upon us one of the most terrific showers of shell and musketry I have ever experienced. My whole line returned the fire and steadily advanced. It was here that our greatest loss occurred, but under all this there was no faltering, no hesitation, and we were soon at the ridge we were ordered to take, the enemy retreating to their rifle pits and shelter behind a stone wall immediately under their batteries. The ridge scarcely afforded us any shelter, except by lying down. Soon after dark the firing on both sides ceased for the night and all was silent, except the moans of the wounded and dying.

At Shiloh, Tennessee, the men of Battery B, First Michigan Light Artillery, stood firm, battling waves of Confederate troops in the Civil War's first bloody battle. This monument marks the spot where the battery was captured by enemy cavalry at the end of the fighting on April 6, 1862.

All that night and the next day the men of the First Division lay in the mud waiting for a Union attack that never came. Burnside had enough. The scene in front of the stone wall, where the slopes were blanketed with dead and wounded, was a grim reminder of the 6,000 Federals that fell that fierce December day. With Stockton's brigade bringing up the rear, Burnside's army recrossed the Rappahannock and another Union disaster passed into history. Although the North suffered repeated setbacks during the first two years of fighting in the east, operations in the west were much more successful. With the help of a Union naval force, an army under General Ulysses S. Grant captured Forts Henry and Donelson in northern Tennessee and advanced to Pittsburg Landing in the southwestern part of the state. At this point Grant seemed to have thought only of attacking the enemy—he positioned his army in an exposed position on the west bank of the Tennessee River without building defensive works. This proved a costly oversight.

On April 6, 1862, a Confederate army hit Grant's advanced units, near Shiloh Church, and a fierce two-day battle began. The Southerners had the element of surprise on their side and took full advantage of it. Throughout the day it seemed only a miracle could prevent the Federals from being pinned against the river and destroyed. But the hard-pressed defenders suffered no such fate, largely because two divisions, one of them commanded by Colonel Benjamin M. Prentiss, tenaciously held their ground in one of the most valorous stands of the war. In Prentiss's division was the Twelfth Michigan under Colonel Francis Quinn, who reported that his men fell back until they arrived at a position covering a main road through the battlefield. Grant's orders were to hold at all hazards. Time after time the Confederates charged, yelling and shooting incessantly at the Federals, who lay on their stomachs behind bushes and trees, returning the fire.

About two o'clock in the afternoon, the Union line bent until it ran at right angles to Prentiss's division, whose left flank was now exposed. The Confederates hit it hard. "Our men were killed at the guns," Quinn recalled, and "the horses were shot in the harness." Late in the day Prentiss ordered the Michigan colonel to rally his regiment, but there was no regiment to rally. As Quinn hunted for his men, he heard heavy firing to the right and rear, telling him that the enemy had completely surrounded the position. Somehow he and a few of his men got out. Quinn soon took command of the division, since Prentiss, along with 2,200 troops had been captured. Survivors of the fight never forgot the buzz and whine of the swarms of rifle balls; it is no wonder that Southerners called the place where Prentiss fought the Hornet's Nest.

Darkness put an end to the fighting. During the night General Don Carlos Buell's Army of the Ohio arrived on the scene. The next day the Federals struck back, driving from the field the enemy that had come close to a smashing victory.

The first great battle of the war, Shiloh was bloody. Nearly 24,000 Americans were killed, wounded or missing, more than the total casualties of the nation's three previous wars: the War for Independence, the War of 1812 and the Mexican War. But greater battles with even greater losses lay ahead.

During the weeks that followed Shiloh, Federal troops in the west were scattered over a broad front. The prospects for a successful offensive against the center of the Union line seemed good. In August 1862

General Braxton Bragg led a Southern army northward through Tennessee with plans to march to the Ohio River. On the way he expected to "liberate" Kentucky, whose citizens he mistakenly thought would greet him with open arms. While Bragg moved north, Confederate forces in Mississippi attempted to join him, but they were met and defeated by Union troops at Iuka and Corinth in the fall of 1862. Two Michigan regiments, the Third Cavalry and the Fifteenth Infantry, saw heavy action in the Iuka-Corinth campaign and were commended by General William Rosecrans for their courage, efficiency and gallantry.

Autumn found Bragg in the heart of Kentucky, where he was given a cool reception by the Kentuckians and a hot one by Buell's Army of the Ohio. Buell, who was plodding southward when Bragg launched his offensive, swung his army north and hit the invaders at Perryville on October 8, 1862. Michigan infantry, cavalry, engineers and mechanics, and artillery fought in that bloody battle. Bragg, stopped in his tracks, was forced to withdraw into Tennessee. Buell, already hotly criticized for allowing the enemy to penetrate deeply into Kentucky, failed to pursue and was dismissed from his command. Buell's army, newly named the Army of the Cumberland, was given to Rosecrans, who concentrated at Nashville. Late in December 1862 he struck at Murfreesboro, 30 miles to the south.

The battle that followed was awful. In penetrating cold, half-paralyzed men fought to the death in the drab cotton fields and soggy cedar brakes that stretched along Stones River. Six regiments of Michigan infantry and one of cavalry saw action in a battle that lost about 12,000 men on each side, nearly one-third of the total number engaged.

The Ninth Michigan must have concluded that Murfreesboro was a place to avoid. Five months earlier a Union force of about brigade strength had been occupying the town. With it were six companies of the Ninth. At dawn on July 13, 1862, Confederate General Nathan Bedford Forrest and about 2,000 cavalry had descended upon Murfreesboro, whipped the outnumbered bluecoats, forcing them to surrender.

Colonel John G. Parkhurst of Coldwater, commander of the Ninth, was, among those taken prisoner. Parkhurst, who had entered service in September 1861, was released after a brief captivity. He returned to what was left of his regiment in time to fight at Stones River, where he and his men were sent to help stop Bragg's daybreak assault against the Union right flank. The attack, nearly swept the Federals from the field, but they managed to form a line that held. Bragg let a whole day slip away before striking again. When he did, the attack was smashed by Federal artillery. That night, Bragg withdrew. Six months passed before the two armies clashed again. When the Federal army marched into Murfreesboro, the Ninth Michigan, its commander at the head, led the way. Parkhurst remembered the occasion as the "proudest day of his life."

Bragg's retreat brought to a close a maximum Confederate effort conducted on three fronts over a four-month period. The armies of Lee, Bragg and Earl Van Dorn had been stopped and turned back at Antietam, Perryville and Corinth. Union counteroffensives had also been stopped cold along the Rappahannock in Virginia and Stones River in Tennessee. What the war had in store for the blue and the gray in 1863 could not be known until spring, when troops would march off to fight again, some to "Dixie," others to the "Battle Hymn of the Republic." Until then the fighting subsided and the soldiers went into winter quarters.

Thirty-nine-year-old Benjamin Fisher left his East Saginaw home on August 9, 1861, to join the Sixteenth Infantry as a captain. Less than one year later he was wounded and taken prisoner at Gaines Mill, Virginia. After his recuperation and exchange he was commissioned major of the Twenty-third Michigan Infantry.

Up Front With
Michigan Soldiers
· · · · · · ·

A rmy life made men prove their mettle in more ways than one. Beyond braving the supreme test of an exploding battlefield, soldiers had to cope with an array of discomforts that accounted for more desertions than the ordeal of combat did. Endless miles of marching—much of it under the worst conditions imaginable—caused leg-weary men to complain and curse while they continued to do all that was asked of them. While campaigning in Kentucky, a Michigan soldier wrote:

> *We marched all day the first day in the rain and mud ankle deep and it was hard I can tell you. However, we went 13 miles the first day, and in the morning a dubious prospect presented itself. The mud was verry deep and thick and it was still raining but it made no odds. We had to start again rain or shine and the last day we went 18 miles. . . . When I got [to] our journey's end I was so stiff I could scarcely stir.*

When winter came, campaigning usually ceased. Except for an occasional crack of a musket or the boom of a gun, stillness settled over the entire front. "All quiet on the Potomac" appeared frequently in the winter entries of a diary kept by a Michigan sergeant. Like his comrades, he was bored with life in winter quarters and grumbled about the foul weather and the lack of anything to do. Rain, sleet and snow often brought things to a standstill and made living conditions miserable. Some found it so monotonous and uncomfortable in the cold drab confines of an army tent that they drank heavily, became quarrelsome and got into fights. In general the soldiers did a variety of things to pass away the time. They washed and sewed their clothes, cleaned their weapons, kept their gear in shape and performed

numerous camp duties. They also played cards, shot dice, read and wrote letters. In the Twenty-third Michigan Infantry a young, card-playing soldier received a scolding letter from his parents, who had somehow got word that their son was gambling. He replied,

> *I do Play euchre once in a while, but not for money. A fellow can sit here in his tent all day and do nothing and it is lonesome. There is no reading to be had except novels and they are scarce, and there is no more harm in playing cards for pastime than there is in playing fox and geese but if you say stop it shall be done and I will go to reading novels because I can't sit still all day long and do nothing.*

Soldiers appreciated the importance of the work they were doing and determined to see it through to a successful conclusion. A Michigan officer lamented to his sweetheart:

> *Oh! that this monstrous rebellion was crushed. But, Darling, before high heaven, I now declare that I want nothing but war, war, death and desolation until we can have an honorable peace. . . . Do not consider me heartless, or unfeeling. 'Tis my love for the land of my birth, my home, my country.*

Bands helped soldiers endure the monotonous and often lonely life in the army. Opposite is the band of the Nineteenth Michigan at McMinnville, Tennessee, in 1862; above is the band of the Twenty-fourth Michigan.

As the war dragged on, soldiers complained more and more about army life. A private in the Twenty-sixth Michigan wrote early in 1863 that he was sick of soldiering, adding, "there is a good meny that has got the same feeling." When a man in the Fourteenth Michigan heard that his son planned to volunteer, he scribbled a message to his wife:

> *Tell him i dont want him to enlist as it is a real dogs life which he will find out after it is to late. . . . i had rather see him go to his grave then to enlist as i no he never can stand it but you need not say so to any boddy els as i dont want to discourage enlistments.*

Another Michigan veteran assured his wife that he was very patriotic but would "disert in a holey minet" if he had the chance. Discontent resulted in part from lack of confidence in superiors, which increased with Union defeats. The diaries and letters of Michigan soldiers—men quick to praise able commanders—contain venomous criticism of the nation's military and political leaders.

John Ryder, who served in the Twenty-fourth Michigan, found army life distasteful, observing on Christmas Day 1862, "I have got just about sick of war . . . this soldiering is a big thing, but I can't see it." Ryder was killed six months later at the Battle of Gettysburg.

The subject of food gave the servicemen plenty to grumble about. Sometimes there was little or nothing to eat. Sometimes, the food they were given was spoiled. A Michigan private informed his wife that his regiment had good coffee and bread, but he complained about the "stinking beef." Attempting to tell her that the diet lacked variety, he wrote that the men had to eat "one thing over and over." During combat soldiers up front often ran out of food. An officer in the Twenty-second Michigan discovered during the siege of Chattanooga that "one can live on corn alone. I fattened on a double hand full of this 'heavy feed' for three days and two nights," he recalled, "and the entire Regt enjoyed the same sumtuous fare, plentifully 'peppered' with Rebel shell."

Frequently, soldiers on the move had to gulp down tasteless food under the most unappetizing conditions imaginable. A Michigan artilleryman remembered a 15-day winter march in which he waded two rivers—the cold water up to his armpits—slept on the ground that night in wet clothes, got up at dawn the next day and marched through rain and swamps until noon, when he "dined" in a mudhole on "a small peace of corn bread made of corn meal and water and a small peace of fresh beef about enough for an old cat." When the opportunity presented itself, some soldiers bought food to supplement their army diet. One Michigan infantryman found prices too high. Disconsolate, he wrote that "a man in the army has no chance to live any beter than a common hog." No wonder the soldiers were delighted when occasionally they were treated to culinary windfalls from foraging expeditions or raiding enemy supply depots.

Horace W. Cummings (left), age 37, and William E. Davis (right), age 18, were two of the nearly 10,000 Michigan men to die of disease during the Civil War.

Throughout the war, disease was a greater killer than enemy fire. Deaths from illness astonished a Michigan private, who noted that "we have lost about thirty by disease since the regiment was organized and have not lost one by the bullet." Every malady from colds and children's diseases to typhoid fever, malaria and smallpox plagued the men in uniform. Among the Michigan soldiers who succumbed from illness, was former governor Moses Wisner, who commanded the Twenty-second Michigan until he died from typhoid fever in early 1863.

For months on end, men were thrown together—often in cramped quarters, exposed to foul weather and wretched conditions and without curative or preventive medicine. Ten Michigan soldiers died from disease to every four killed by enemy action. It is little wonder that those at home worried endlessly about their loved ones in the service.

To relieve the anxiety of fretful friends and relatives, soldiers often began their letters with a few words about their health. These were usually followed by an expression of hope that all at home were well. A Michigan man, opening one of his letters in this manner, penned an amusing message to his brother: "I am well at present with the exception that I have got a Dyerear now and I hope theas few lines will find you the same."

On April 27, 1865, the *Sultana*, a steamship carrying more than 2,200 Union soldiers, sank in the Mississippi River. Among the more than 1,600 men who drowned in the nation's worst maritime disaster were 68 members of the Eighteenth Michigan Infantry.

Scores of Michigan men were injured or killed in accidents. Carelessness while handling weapons was the greatest single cause of mishaps. Michigan soldiers were also victims of such accidents as drowning, being thrown or kicked by horses and falling from or being hit by trains or wagons. The most costly noncombat disaster involving Michigan men occurred on the Mississippi River. Union soldiers who had been captured then paroled were returning home aboard the *Sultana*. Near Memphis, Tennessee, on April 27, 1865, the steamship blew up. Sixty-eight men of the Eighteenth Michigan lost their lives.

Exposed daily to the grim realities of war, the soldiers often dreamt of happier times. Inevitably they thought of home. Many fell into the clutches of that wretched ailment whose only sure remedy could not be had, whose vicious spell tore mightily at the hearts of men who were lonesome in the midst of thousands. One downcast youngster in the

Twenty-second Michigan expressed this loneliness simply: "If a boy was ever home-sick, it is me."

The balm that soothed the aching hearts of homesick soldiers was a letter from home. "You must write," "Be sure to write" and "I want to hear from you" were phrases that appeared in almost every letter that servicemen sent home. A teenage Michigan infantryman who had gone for several days without word from his parents sent them a mild and almost pathetic rebuke:

You must write to me once a week and I will do the same by you. You may not get all of my letters but you are at home and hapyer than I can make myself in the Army and you will not miss the letters if you dont get them every week as much as I shall if I dont get mine from you.

Holland resident Jan Wilterdink, who served with the Twenty-fifth Michigan Infantry, noted, "The war makes a decent person forget his Christian upbringing."

Mostly, the soldiers wanted to know how their loved ones at home were getting along. A Michigan officer expressed the sentiment of multitudes when he wrote: "You can only guess how much good it does one in the army to get letters."

Servicemen also turned to the folks at home for food, clothing and various articles. In a typical request, one young private asked his

Eighteen-year-old Thaddeus Southworth of Hillsdale County enlisted in the Second Michigan Cavalry in October 1861. Illness eventually forced him to leave the army in August 1862.

Michigan parents to send him a box with dried plums, honey, jelly, cherries, apples, dried currants and "a nice bottle of linament." Stamps were usually scarce on the front lines. Requests for stamps were numerous, especially after soldiers had missed one or more paydays.

The men in the ranks worried about those they left behind and frequently sent them words of encouragement. In spring 1862 a Michigan infantryman tried to boost the morale of his parents by a display of optimism. "Keep up good courage," he wrote, "for I have faith to believe that we shall be at home to spend the fourth of July." Most of the troops were confident that they were "agoing to get out of this fight all right."

A religious note often crept into letters discussing survival. Many soldiers expressed a belief that there existed a definite connection between clean living and surviving the war. One devout Michigan veteran, hospitalized by illness, informed his parents that he owned a pocket-sized Bible. "I shall read it," he promised, "and try and lead a

James Bendle mustered into the Sixth Michigan Cavalry on January 5, 1864. Within a month the 19-year-old took ill. He died on March 12 at Brandy Station, Virginia.

good life and put my trust [in]God for he can carry me safely through if my trust is in him for he says he is merciful to all and he will be if they seek him."

Such expressions of faith must have had a solacing effect on those at home who hoped and prayed for an early peace and the safe return of their fighting men. But the war dragged on.

While most Michigan units in the Western Theater were besieged at Chattanooga in November 1863, five Michigan regiments were hotly engaged with Confederate forces near Knoxville, Tennessee. Leading the Twenty-third Michigan was Colonel Marshall W. Chapin of Detroit. During the campaign the normally healthy Chapin claimed he was ill and left the field. He left the army in spring 1864 after being severely criticized for his actions at Knoxville.

A Civil War Soldiers' Album

· · · · · · ·

Thousands of soldiers, like this unidentified young man of the First Michigan Engineers and Mechanics, had their pictures taken to give to proud and anxious loved ones. Today, many of the names of men whose images adorn *cartes de visite* and tintypes are lost to history.

The First Michigan Infantry was formed from state militia companies. The largest company, known as the Detroit Light Guard, became Company A when the regiment left for
Washington DC in 1861. This Light Guard private displays full marching gear.

The Seventeenth Michigan Infantry saw its first action at the Battle of South Mountain, Maryland, on September 14, 1862. In fierce fighting the Seventeenth, which earned for its actions the nickname the Stonewall Regiment, suffered 141 casualties. Members of this unit included (clockwise from upper left) William B. Hurd, Simpson T. Clark, Walter G. Bigsby and Orson B. Woodin. All four survived the war, although Hurd, who entered the war in 1861 as a private in the First Michigan Infantry, spent a year in a Southern prison after his capture at Spotsylvania.

Thirteen-year-old Robert H. Hendershot, a drummer boy with the Eighth Michigan Infantry, crossed the Rappahannock River before Fredericksburg on December 11, 1862, clinging to the side of a pontoon boat. He grabbed onto the boat after men of the Seventh Michigan refused to allow him to join them in an expedition to roust rebels from the city. Dubbed the Drummer Boy of the Rappahannock, Hendershot received for his actions this engraved silver drum from *New York Tribune* editor Horace Greeley.

Bryan Root Pierce, who moved to Grand Rapids from New York in 1856, entered service as a captain of the Third Michigan Infantry in 1861. Of the five wounds Pierce sustained during the war, his third—inflicted at Gettysburg—eventually cost him his leg. Pierce commanded a brigade and occasionally a division during the 1864 Virginia Campaign. Breveted a major general, he left the service in August 1865. Pierce was Michigan's last surviving Civil War general, dying on July 10, 1924, at the age of 95.

These unidentified officers served with the Twenty-third Michigan Infantry, which was mustered into service at Saginaw in September 1862. The Twenty-third saw extensive action in the 1864 Atlanta Campaign.

Disguised as Franklin Thompson, Sarah E. Edmonds of Flint, enlisted in the Second Michigan Infantry in 1861. Edmonds deserted in 1863 after she contracted malaria and feared doctors would discover her true identity. After the war she published her war experiences, received a pension and has the distinction of being the only woman ever granted membership in the Grand Army of the Republic.

George E. Judd of Grand Rapids (above, with his wife and children) entered the Third Michigan Infantry in June 1861. He lost his left arm in fighting at Fair Oaks, Virginia, in 1862.

During the Battle of Gettysburg the Twenty-fourth Michigan lost 22 of its 25 officers; among them was newly promoted Captain Richard S. Dillon, who was severely wounded in the leg. He recuperated, returned to his command and was mustered out in 1865.

Only five Northern states sent more regiments of cavalry to the Union army than Michigan. Organized in Grand Rapids in mid-1863, the Tenth Michigan Cavalry was actively engaged in Tennessee during 1864. It did not return to the state until mid-November 1865. Its officers included (clockwise from upper left) Captain Edwin J. Brooks of Leelanau, Captain James L. Smith of Plainfield (who entered the war as a private in the Eighth New York Infantry), Major Harvey E. Light of Eureka and Second Lieutenant Sam White Jr. of Grand Rapids.

On the afternoon of July 3, 1863, recently pro-moted Captain Samuel Hodgman of Climax (above) and the Seventh Michigan Infantry were positioned at the center of the Union line, near a small clump of trees. Following a two-hour rebel artillery barrage of their position, these Michiganians and their comrades on Cemetery Ridge witnessed one of the war's most awesome spectacles as approximately 14,000 rebels moved out of the trees about a mile away and marched across the open fields. Northern cannon and muskets exacted a dreadful toll. The rebels pushed on, but only several hundred reached their destination—the Copse of Trees (left). The fighting became hand-to-hand. Hodgman later recalled, "We stuck to our barricade and fought till they—what were left of them—were glad to come into our lines or skedaddle double quick." Hodgman was uninjured, but the Seventh suf-fered one-third casualties.

Born in Quincy, Michigan, in 1843, Smith Hastings went off to war with the First Michigan Infantry in 1861. In August 1862 he joined the Fifth Michigan Cavalry as a captain. In 1893 a fellow officer protested to the War Department that the war's official records failed to give Hastings credit for his actions at a skirmish at Newby's Cross Roads, Virginia, on July 24, 1863. In disobedience to orders, 19-year-old Hastings aided members of Battery M, Second U.S. Artillery, defending their guns as they engaged Confederates. Hastings received the Medal of Honor in 1897.

Michigan's 67 congressional Medal of Honor winners included (clockwise from upper left) German-born Conrad Noll, who seized the colors of an enemy regiment at Spotsylvania in May 1864; 19-year-old Thomas Custer, George Custer's brother, who received two medals for capturing two rebel flags in early April 1865; Alonzo Smith, who captured the flag of the Twenty-sixth North Carolina Infantry in October 1864 at Hatcher's Run, Virginia; and Frank D. Baldwin, who "singly" entered the enemy's line and captured two officers and "a guidon of a Georgia regiment" at Peachtree Creek, Georgia, in July 1864. After the war, Baldwin, then serving in the U.S. Army, received a second Medal of Honor for saving two hostages from their Indian captors in Texas in 1874.

Famed Civil War photographer Mathew Brady took these six photographs of the Fourth Michigan Infantry. Unlike most Civil War units, the Fourth, which mustered into service in Adrian in June 1861, suffered more casualties on the battlefield than from disease.

In 1864 Philippines native Felix Balderberry (top) joined the Eleventh Michigan Infantry. Hiram R. Ellis (right) of Saugatuck first served with the Fifth Michigan Cavalry, then later joined the Twenty-eighth Michigan Infantry, where he was adjutant. William Eagle of Clinton County (above) served with the Third Michigan Cavalry.

Fifteen-year-old Thomas H. Grant of Detroit enlisted in the Fourteenth Michigan Infantry on February 15, 1862. In March 1864 he was discharged and traveled to Buffalo, New York, where, under the name of Thomas Davis, he enlisted in the Fifth New York Heavy Artillery. While fighting with that unit, Grant was captured at Cedar Creek, Virginia, on October 19, 1864. After spending several months in a Richmond Prison, he was discharged in June 1865 and returned to Detroit.

Organized in Paw Paw by William H. Hugo, the Lafayette Light Guard (top) was unable to find a Michigan regiment in which to serve, so it traveled to New York and became Company C, Seventieth New York Infantry. Above, an unidentified Michigan soldier poses with his array of weapons, including a unique Colt revolving rifle.

These men served in the Sixth Michigan Infantry. Clockwise from upper left, Charles S. Fassett of Sandstone was wounded at Baton Rouge, Louisiana, in August 1862; Edward Bacon of Niles, who joined the Sixth in June 1861, commanded the regiment by early 1864; James Brainerd of Eaton Rapids died in Louisiana in mid-1864; and Andrew Merrill of Berrien County was the Sixth's quartermaster sergeant.

Nineteen-year-old First Lieutenant Charles W. Calkins (left) and 21-year-old Captain Joseph C. Herkner (right), both from Grand Rapids, entered the First Michigan Engineers and Mechanics in 1861. Both men survived the war. In four years of campaigning, the First Engineers provided valuable service to the Union cause.

The Triumph of
Union Arms

• • • • • • •

After Burnside's defeat at Fredericksburg, the Army of the Potomac got a new commander, General Joseph Hooker, who opened an offensive in April 1863. Hooker claimed that his force of 120,000 men, which included seven Michigan regiments, was "the finest army on the planet." He was probably right—what it needed was an able commander. That it did not have one became evident to many during the Battle of Chancellorsville (May 1-4, 1863), when, at the crucial hour, Hooker was found wanting in both ability and moral courage. Hooker's intention was to trap Lee in Fredericksburg, then crush him in the jaws of a Union vise. But the wily Confederate commander, refusing to be caught, demonstrated in front of Hooker and held his huge army at bay, while Stonewall Jackson's divisions made a wide sweep to the west and came in on the exposed Union right flank. Jackson's late afternoon attack hurled back regiments, brigades and divisions, one upon another. Units that had advanced against Lee, among them the Third Michigan Infantry, pulled back to avoid being cut off. Finding their way partially blocked by an enemy force, they made a bayonet attack in the black of night and succeeded in getting through to the main army.

When the Union right caved in under Jackson's blow, General George Meade ordered the First Division of his Fifth Corps to take and hold the high ground toward where the Confederates were heading. The division commander called on the Fourth and Sixteenth Michigan Infantries to carry out the order. They seized and held the position, establishing a battle line that the routed Union soldiers could rally behind. The First and Fifth Michigan Infantries were also engaged in severe fighting. The First skirmished with Confederate pickets the afternoon before the main armies clashed, fought up front throughout the struggle and helped bring up the rear during the Union army retreat. The brigade in which the First served was marched and counter-marched so often during the six-day battle that it became known as the Flying Brigade. But the efforts of the hard-fighting Federals ended in defeat because of incompetence at the top. The battle turned out to be a monstrous sacrifice of soldiers who deserved a better fate. Colonel Ira C. Abbott, commander of the First Michigan, displayed remarkable restraint when he wrote in his official report that "for all that tests the quality of a soldier [Chancellorsville] surpasses all our former experience."

After the battle, Lee made the momentous decision to invade the North a second time. A bold stroke might help the South diplomatically, destroy Union morale, increase war-weariness in the North and force Grant, who was thundering away at Vicksburg, to send troops to the east, thereby relieving the besieged Confederates in that Mississippi city. Swinging his army into the Shenandoah Valley, Lee struck northward, crossed the Potomac River and by the end of June 1863 had about 75,000 men in southern Pennsylvania. On June 28 Lincoln announced that he had relieved Hooker and appointed Meade to command the Army of the Potomac, then numbering about 90,000 men.

On the day that Meade took over the army, a Pennsylvania community soon to become famous, buzzed with excitement. A few days earlier several gray-clad regiments had passed through Gettysburg. Now soldiers from the Army of the Potomac entered the town amid a royal reception. People filled the streets, cheered, shouted greetings and words of praise, tossed flowers and gave the smiling cavalrymen and their horses food and drink. The troopers of the Fifth and Sixth regiments of the Michigan Cavalry Brigade long remembered the warmth with which the people of Gettysburg welcomed them that last Sunday of June 1863. Two days later General John Buford's cavalry clashed with Confederate infantry, raising the curtain on the greatest battle of the war. Serving in the Union army at Gettysburg were seven regiments of Michigan infantry and five of cavalry. Some of these organizations were in the worst fighting of those memorable days in early July.

On the morning of July 1, 1863, Union cavalrymen struggled to hold a ridge west of Gettysburg against advancing enemy infantry. South of town, the leading regiments of the Army of the Potomac's First Corps, came up the Emmitsburg Road, cut across the fields to where the fighting was going on and deployed along the ridge. The black-hatted Midwesterners of the crack Iron Brigade were on the job.

With that famous organization was the Twenty-fourth Michigan Infantry, one of the state's finest Civil War regiments. It was recruited in a hurry, drew most of its men from Wayne County and was honored by one of those florid ceremonies that usually attended a regiment's departure from Michigan. Appropriate speeches centered on the presentation of a handsome flag—"red, white, and blue in stars of raised work"—and an inscription that read "24th Michigan Infantry." After the colors were presented to the regiment, Colonel Henry A. Morrow, the commanding officer, made a brief patriotic speech. Late that August the Twenty-fourth left Michigan, and after spending a month in forts near Washington DC, they marched to Sharpsburg, Maryland, and joined the Iron Brigade. The Battle of Antietam had just been fought and the green Michigan soldiers had the awesome experience of marching across the battlefield, where shell-torn earth, charred buildings, splintered trees, a huge pile of amputated arms and legs, and freshly filled graves silently bespoke an epic to which the Twenty-fourth would contribute gloriously.

The new men got a cold reception from the soldiers with whom they were brigaded. The veterans resented the rookie regiment whose 900 men, wearing regulation forage caps, equaled in number the total of the other four regiments in the unit. Moreover, word had gone around that the newcomers were bounty men. This notion—a mistaken one—was another reason why the hard-bitten warriors of the Iron Brigade were aloof. Until the Michigan men proved their worth, the veterans of the brigade would have little or nothing to do with them. Two months later, during the Battle of Fredericksburg, the Twenty-fourth performed like seasoned soldiers, finally winning their comrades respect. Subsequently, the Michigan soldiers appeared for the first time wearing

This woodcut (top) depicts the Iron Brigade contesting the advancing Confederates in McPherson's Woods on July 1, 1863, at Gettysburg. On that day, Henry A. Morrow, commander of the Twenty-fourth Michigan, was wounded.

the headdress the brigade had made famous, a black Hardee pattern army hat. "Those damned black hats," cursed the Confederates, an oath signifying not contempt but respect for men who fought hard.

West of Gettysburg, the Iron Brigade swung into action. General James Archer's rebels, who expected to find Pennsylvania militia in front of them, were heard to exclaim: "Here are those damned black-hat fellers again. 'Tain't no militia—that's the Army of the Potomac!" Like enraged animals the veteran brigades came together. Two Wisconsin regiments hit Archer's men head-on, while the Twenty-fourth Michigan and the Nineteenth Indiana struck their right flank. The Confederates broke in confusion and scampered for higher ground to the west, leaving behind many prisoners that included General Archer.

Time was vital. The Southern army was nearer than the Army of the Potomac and approaching fast. The Iron Brigade had beaten back the enemy advance, but there was no time to gloat over it. Confederate General Ambrose P. Hill poured his men into the struggle. In the early afternoon heat, the Southern line surged forward, driving the Federals back. Darkness found the shattered remnants of an entire Union corps on the high ground south of Gettysburg, about a mile from the Lutheran seminary near where the fighting had begun.

When the Confederate drive started, the Iron Brigade occupied a position near the seminary, with orders to hold out as long as possible. It stood its ground until the enemy closed in and began slugging it from three sides, then the outnumbered black hats withdrew. The retreat was treacherous, and had to be made through a corridor formed by converging enemy battle lines—the Federals were severely mauled before they got out. The Iron Brigade had gone into the fight with 1,800 effectives; it came out with less than 650. It had fought its last great fight.

The Twenty-fourth Michigan had entered the conflict with its regimental colors in the hands of Sergeant Abel Peck. Three months earlier Peck had written his daughter that "some of the men did not think the Army of the Potomac would have much to do during the coming summer." Now, as his regiment crossed Willoughby Run, a bullet came out of the smoke that hung low in the ravine, killing him. Others were hit before the regiment reached a wooded area offering momentary respite. Then, like "yelling demons," the Confederates rushed in, got on the Twenty-fourth's flank and pounded the Michigan men with all they had. Three color bearers were cut down. A fourth, Corporal Andrew Wagner, heard Colonel Morrow's command to plant the flagstaff in the ground for a rally but Wagner fell with a bullet in his breast before doing so. Morrow grabbed the colors, but Private William Kelly took it from him, saying, "the Colonel of the Twenty-fourth shall never carry the flag while I am alive." Then Kelly was hit and killed instantly. Another private took the flag, but when a bullet knocked him down, the colonel again grabbed the colors. Then he was hit and had to leave the field.

Members of the Twenty-fourth Michigan Infantry included (clockwise from upper left) Surgeon John H. Beech, Chaplain William C. Way, Captain William Hutchinson who was wounded at Gettysburg, and Color Sergeant Abel G. Peck, who was killed at Gettysburg.

The regiment was being so severely mauled that the new commander ordered a retreat. The Michigan men fell back, fighting as they went. Of the 496 men who entered the fight that morning, 399 were killed, wounded or missing by nightfall. The Twenty-fourth's casualty list was the longest of any Union regiment that fought at Gettysburg. But the unit's magnificent effort had helped gain time for the Federal army to close in and occupy the strong position from which it was destined to deliver a crippling blow to Lee's army.

On the second day of Gettysburg, five Michigan regiments took part in the struggle for Big Round Top and Little Round Top, two vital knolls on the left flank of the Union army. During the terrible fight for those mounds of earth, a strong Confederate force hit and broke the Fifth Michigan, while not far distant the men of the Fourth Michigan saw their commander run through with a bayonet as he tried to save the regimental colors. In the tangled underbrush that covered the boulder-strewn approaches to Little Round Top, the Sixteenth Michigan fought desperately to hold its position. At one point the regiment broke and fell back in confusion, but when support arrived, a new line formed. As the Southerners closed in, wild, blind fighting broke out, bayonets flashed, clubbed muskets cracked skulls and men punched, wrestled and hurled stones dug out of the ground at the enemy. When it finally ended long after dark, the Union had possession of Big and Little Round Tops.

The Battle of Gettysburg climaxed on the afternoon of July 3, 1863, when General George Pickett led 13,000 Virginians and North Carolinians against the center of the Union line. On Cemetery Ridge the men of the Seventh Michigan, veterans of hard campaigning, hugged the ground behind their breastworks during the earthshaking bombardment that preceded the charge. When the guns quieted, the Michigan soldiers, looking westward into the mid-afternoon sun, saw Pickett's well-dressed ranks approaching and braced themselves for the blow. Every step of the way the Confederates took a terrible pounding from Union artillery. Great gaps opened in their columns as men went down ten and twenty at a time. But on they came. A major in the Seventh reported that his men held their fire until the enemy was just yards away, then opened with murderous volleys that knocked the Confederates down in scores. "Many of the enemy," the major noted, "crawled on their hands and feet under the sheet of fire, and coming up to our lines, surrendered themselves prisoners."

According to Major James Kidd (above) of Ionia, George A. Custer (left) was "the most picturesque figure" in the war. Custer took command of the Michigan Cavalry Brigade several days before the Battle of Gettysburg.

Lt. Col. Amos A. Steele, the Seventh's commanding officer, moved his men to smash the enemy's right flank, but a bullet pierced his brain before the maneuver was completed. In the fighting on the summit of the hill a private in the Seventh shot a Confederate flag bearer and grabbed the colors. As the Michigan soldier loaded his musket, with the flag by his side, a Union colonel rode up and demanded the flag, "threatening to cut him down if he did not give it up." The unidentified officer rode off with a prize he did not deserve. At the high tide of the attack a few Confederates pierced the Union line, but Pickett's ranks were decimated and the defeated Southerners fell back on Seminary Ridge.

Throughout the battle Union and Confederate cavalry fought several engagements, the most important of which raged during Pickett's charge. Union success in these clashes can be explained in part by the heroics of the Michigan Cavalry Brigade. Consisting of the First, Fifth, Sixth and Seventh regiments, the brigade was led by Michigan's most colorful Civil War soldier, George Armstrong Custer, just promoted from captain to brigadier general.

Most of the brigade first saw Custer in Hanover, just east of Gettysburg, where a blistering cavalry fight took place on June 30. As they dismounted and closed in to attack, the Michigan soldiers heard an unfamiliar voice directing them. Major James H. Kidd of the Sixth Michigan Cavalry looked closely at the man giving the orders and later described what he saw:

An officer superbly mounted.... Tall, lithe, active, muscular, straight as an Indian and as quick in his movements, he had the fair complexion of a school girl. He was clad in a suit of black velvet elaborately trimmed with gold lace, which ran down the outer seams of his trousers, and almost covered the sleeves of his cavalry jacket. The wide collar of a navy blue shirt was turned down over the collar of his velvet jacket, and a necktie of brilliant crimson was tied in a graceful knot at the throat, the long ends falling carelessly in front. The double rows of buttons on his breast were arranged in groups of twos, indicating the rank of brigadier general. A soft, black hat with wide brim adorned with a gilt cord, and rosette encircling a silver star, was worn turned down on one side giving him a rakish air. His golden hair fell in graceful luxuriance nearly or quite to his shoulders, and his upper lip was garnished with a blonde mustache. A sword and belt, gilt spurs and top boots completed his unique outfit.

Custer and his brigade—one regiment and several other companies armed with Spencer seven-shot repeating rifles, which gave them tremendous firepower—helped drive General James Ewell Brown "Jeb" Stuart's cavalry out of Hanover and away from Lee's army, where it was sorely needed. Stuart had to make a wide sweep to the north in order to get to Lee, but before he got there, he was again engaged. Spearheaded by Custer's brigade, with the Sixth Michigan up front, Union troopers fought Stuart on July 2, 1863, near Hunterstown and delayed his arrival. Stuart's absence, prolonged by Union cavalry, seriously handicapped Lee in the fight at Gettysburg.

On July 3 Stuart and his troops attempted to strike the center of the Union line from the rear while Pickett hit it from the front. Union cavalry intercepted Stuart. In the fight that followed, the men of the Michigan Cavalry Brigade distinguished themselves in magnificent stands and heroic attacks. The outcome was in doubt for hours. Finally, the Southerners gave ground and, unable to get to the Union line, broke off the fighting. Had they succeeded in their mission the great battle might well have ended differently. Their failure was due partly to the effectiveness of Custer's brigade, which lost nearly one-third of the total casualties suffered by Union cavalry at Gettysburg.

The early days of July 1863 also saw the approaching climax of another campaign. In the spring of 1862 the Confederates had lost New Orleans and Memphis, but through the rest of the year and on into the next they had repulsed Union attempts to take Vicksburg, Mississippi. Located on a high bluff overlooking a broad sweep of the Mississippi River, the city was a veritable fortress. Its capture would give the Union control of the great river to its mouth and would split the Confederacy in two. Late in March 1863 General Grant opened a bold and imaginative campaign. By late May they had Vicksburg completely invested. Shortly thereafter seven Michigan regiments arrived as reinforcements and participated in the 45-day siege, which ended on July 4 with the surrender of more than 30,000 Confederates. On its eighty-seventh birthday, a joyous nation celebrated the decisive Union victories of Vicksburg and Gettysburg.

The battlefront extended from the Atlantic coast to the Mississippi River and beyond. In its center lay the city of Chattanooga, Tennessee. Situated on the left bank of the Tennessee River and flanked on the south and east by Missionary Ridge and Lookout Mountain,

Battery A, First Michigan Light Artillery, better known as Loomis's Battery, suffered heavily at the Battle of Chickamauga, where half of its men were killed, wounded or captured.

Chattanooga was an important railroad center, "the transportation solar plexus of the Western Confederacy." In the summer of 1863 the Army of the Cumberland under Rosecrans launched a campaign against Bragg's Confederate army in Chattanooga. With clever maneuvering they forced the Confederates out of the city without a battle. About the time Bragg received reinforcements, Rosecrans moved against him. The two armies clashed in the Battle of Chickamauga in northwestern Georgia. Eight Michigan regiments—six infantry and two cavalry—and Batteries A and D, First Light Artillery, and the First Engineers and Mechanics took part in the action.

Chickamauga was the end of the road for many soldiers in Battery A, First Michigan Light Artillery. Known throughout the war as Loomis's Battery, this unit, organized in Coldwater, mustered into the service in late May 1861. Its commander was Captain Cyrus O. Loomis. Until Chickamauga the battery's greatest combat experience occurred at Perryville, where the Michigan artillerymen were ordered to hold, at all costs, a key position on the field. Hiram Lyons, the battery's "long-haired color bearer," recalled how the Michigan gunners, without adequate infantry support, "stood by the pieces and repelled five charges, the enemy at times being able to touch the muzzles of the guns." The

Approximately 450 feet long and 58 feet high, the Elk River Bridge in Tennessee, was built in eight days by the First Michigan Engineers and Mechanics.

battery's salvos mowed down great swaths of yelling Confederates, and the artillerymen successfully held their ground.

At Chickamauga the battery, commanded by Lieutenant George W. Van Pelt of Coldwater, was attached to General George Thomas's Fourteenth Corps. Since the Confederate battle plan called for an assault on the Union left—held by the Fourteenth Corps—Thomas's front boiled with action from the start. As the first day of the battle dawned the Michigan gunners arrived on the field, unlimbered their pieces and commenced firing. While the guns boomed, hordes of yelling Confederates charged; the battery was lashed with musketry and canister. Most of the gunners held their position, firing until they fell or were captured. A war correspondent wrote that when the Confederates closed in, Van Pelt drew his sword and shouted, "Don't dare touch these guns." Then he was killed. The attackers overran and nearly anni-hilated the battery, killing, wounding or capturing about half of the men, slaying 40 of their horses and capturing five of the six guns. Later in the battle, Union troops recovered the lost guns, one of which now stands in a park in Coldwater, as a tribute to men who deserve to be remembered.

The victorious Confederates promptly placed the Army of the Cumberland under siege in Chattanooga. In November, after being penned up for nearly two months, a Michigan soldier in Battery D, First Light Artillery, described conditions in the city, writing he was "well and in good spirits" but had been "poorly fed" since Chickamauga. For three days at a time, he wrote, Union soldiers subsisted "wholy on Parched Corn and since the 20th of September we have not at any time had more than 3/4 Rations and most of the time 1/2 Rations." He told how the Confederates on Missionary Ridge and Lookout Mountain kept the city under fire. "The report of a Reb Canon and bursting of a shell over our heads is so common that we fail to notice it, for it happens every hour in the day."

By the time that letter was written, the worst was over—a supply line had been opened into the city. This monumental operation was accomplished by Union engineers and infantrymen. Erecting a sawmill, they cut lumber, built a steamboat and opened the so-called cracker line into Chattanooga. At the same time, they built a pontoon bridge and a road so supplies could be sent to the besieged troops. Soldiers of the First Michigan Engineers and Mechanics played a prominent role in this work. With the help of Michigan infantrymen, they emplaced the pontoon bridge, known as the Michigan Bridge, which spanned the Tennessee River. In recognition of their accomplishments General Thomas commended the men for their "skill and cool gallantry" in executing their important assignment.

Supplies and reinforcements poured into Chattanooga in preparation for an offensive. General Grant, now in command of the entire Western Theater, was on hand to direct the operations. A Michigan soldier, grasping the significance of this activity, summed it up simply: "As soon as our men get a lot of Hard Tack up here I think we will push on to Atlanta. . . . Then look out for another *big fight*."

Although the push to Atlanta was months away, Grant opened his campaign late in November 1863. The Battle of Chattanooga (November 23-25) was a decisive Union victory that eight Michigan regiments helped win. During the main phase of the struggle, the Eleventh

Michigan Infantry joined in one of the most spectacular charges of the war. The Eleventh, which mustered into Federal service in December 1861, had taken part in rugged campaigning in Kentucky and Tennessee. Under Colonel William L. Stoughton of Sturgis, the regiment had fought in Thomas's corps at Chickamauga and was one of the last units to leave the field.

Along with their comrades, the men of the Eleventh, smarting over their defeat and the hardships endured during the siege of Chattanooga, wanted revenge. Their opportunity came on the afternoon of November 25 when four divisions, including the one to which they were attached, were ordered to advance and take the rifle pits at the foot of Missionary Ridge. The troops moved forward, drove the enemy out of the trenches, and, without further orders, started climbing the slope in hot pursuit. From the ridge a torrent of canister and bullets hit the Federals; halfway up the rugged height the Eleventh's commanding officer and two color bearers were killed. Captain Patrick H. Keegan took over the regiment and led it to the summit. For a long time after the battle the men of the Eleventh argued with other soldiers about which unit won the race to the summit. One thing was certain—the Eleventh was among the first. Equally certain was that the Confederacy had been dealt another crippling blow.

At the end of 1863 the Union could look back on three decisive victories: Gettysburg, Vicksburg and Chattanooga. At Gettysburg, Lee's

In November 1863, with "skill and cool gallantry," the First Michigan Engineers and the Twenty-second Michigan Infantry built a pontoon bridge over the Tennessee River. Dubbed the Michigan Bridge, it enabled supplies and men to reach the besieged Federals in Chattanooga. This 1863 image, taken after the Battle of Chattanooga, shows the river from Lookout Mountain.

army had been handled so roughly that it never waged another offensive campaign. The capture of Vicksburg divided the Confederacy and gave the Union control of the Mississippi River. The Confederate rout at Chattanooga left the Federals holding all of Tennessee and in position to carry the war to the heart of the South. Overall, these decisive victories boosted Union morale, spelled defeat for Southern diplomacy, stripped the Confederacy of valuable economic resources and demoralized its people.

During the last great phase of the war, Union armies assumed the offensive on all fronts, conducting campaigns that opened in the spring of 1864 and continued, in one form or another, until the collapse of the Confederacy in April 1865. Throughout these operations command of the Union armies was in the hands of General Grant, who headquartered with the Army of the Potomac. General William T. Sherman, commanding in the west, used the winter months to build and train his Union forces. When spring came and Grant moved against Lee in Virginia, Sherman turned his back on Chattanooga and

Mustered in September 1862, the Twenty-first Michigan Infantry saw its first fighting at Perryville, Kentucky. It also fought at Stones River, Chickamauga and Chattanooga. In November 1864 the unit, along with seven other Michigan regiments and two batteries of artillery, participated in William Tecumseh Sherman's famed March to the Sea. At Bentonville, North Carolina, one of the war's last large battles, the Twenty-first suffered heavy casualties. The pictures above show the Twenty-first at quieter times.

headed for Atlanta. The retreating Confederates resisted stubbornly as they withdrew through the mountains of northwestern Georgia. A soldier in the Twenty-third Michigan Infantry wrote that the Federals were skirmishing with the enemy's rear guard every day. Recounting his experiences during the Battle of Resaca (May 13-16, 1864), he said:

> *It was a verry hot place. There was a perfect hail of shot and shell and bullets. We were engaged from one o'clock in the afternoon until dark and lost in killed, wounded and missing 68 men-15 killed and the rest wounded and missing.*

The Tenth and Fourteenth Michigan Infantry regiments, having distinguished themselves in several fierce encounters, were warmly praised in the official reports of brigade, division and corps commanders. On September 1, 1864, when the Confederates evacuated Atlanta, the Fourteenth broke the enemy line at Jonesboro and captured several guns, a Confederate general and his staff, the colors of a rebel regiment and 300 soldiers. By that time 15 Michigan regiments had joined in what was one of the most trying and significant campaigns of the war. The capture of Atlanta helped Lincoln win the presidency for a second term and put Sherman in position to make his devastating March to the Sea.

Although Atlanta had fallen, General John Hood's Confederate army remained intact. When Sherman headed for the coast, Hood began operating on his rear in an effort to divert him. Expecting such a move, Sherman sent Thomas back to Nashville to hold the Union center and protect his lines of communication. The first great clash between the opposing forces occurred at Franklin, south of the Tennessee capital, on November 30, 1864. In a frontal assault against strong Union entrenchments, Hood hurled 18,000 troops—more men than had charged with Pickett at Gettysburg. It was a Confederate blood bath. One Michigan private recalled how the rebels "charged our works some twelve to fourteen times and were repulsed every time with heavy slaughter. . . . There were very few killed in our Regt as we had good breastworks." In the Battle of Franklin the Union lost more than 2,000 troops; the Confederacy lost more than 6,000 men.

Two weeks later, at Nashville the two armies met again. When Hood

One of the Union army's most unique units, the Michigan Cavalry Brigade included the First, Fifth, Sixth and Seventh regiments. At Falling Waters, Maryland, on July 14, 1863, the Sixth Michigan Cavalry (top) attacked Robert E. Lee's retreating army. Above are officers of the Michigan Cavalry Brigade.

arrived outside the city he threw up earthworks and made a pretense of besieging Nashville. On December 15, Thomas struck. Hood's thin line crumbled under sledgehammer blows by Union infantry and cavalry. The Southerners were put to flight. Two of the five Michigan regiments at Nashville were cavalry units, the Second and the Eighth; they participated in one of the most relentless pursuits of the war. When it was over, Hood's army ceased to exist as an effective fighting machine. Nashville was a smashing Union victory.

A week later Sherman completed his march across Georgia, entering Savannah on December 22, 1864. From there a soldier in one of the eight Michigan regiments that marched with Sherman wrote that orders to forage had been carried out with a vengeance. "We had fresh pork, chickens, turkeys, geese, ducks and all sutch in the meat line, and for bread we yoused flower and meal that we got from the inhabitants on the way and all the sweet potatoes we could eat and some huney and butter." Behind them was a devastated area 60 miles wide and 250 miles long. There had been much needless destruction, but more was to come. In January 1865 Sherman's army left Savannah and headed north.

While Sherman advanced through the Carolinas, Grant was tightening his grip on Lee's army at Richmond in the final phase of a campaign that had been launched the previous spring—a campaign in which 18 Michigan regiments took part. In battle after battle the fighting was horrid and the suffering cruel.

There was the Battle of the Wilderness on May 5-6, 1864, when angry men fought in a jungle of scrubs and tangled vines, so dense that enemy troops seemed to come out of nowhere only yards away. It was where bullets whined through smoke-filled air and exploding shells tore through the heavy growth, shattering the men struggling to get through and where fires broke out, trapping fallen soldiers, who screamed in agony as the flames consumed their disabled bodies. It was where the men of the Eighth Michigan Infantry charged the enemy with bayonets, only to be cut off and pounded mercilessly, losing their commander and nearly 100 men before getting out.

The Wilderness was followed by fighting at Spotsylvania (May 7-20), where the soldiers of the Seventeenth Michigan Infantry, cheered by their comrades, rushed a hill and forced enemy troops to abandon a position from which they had threatened the flank of a Union brigade. It was where the same regiment, the next day, charged against vastly superior numbers and was broken, losing about 190 of the 225 men that made the attack.

Wounded and taken prisoner in the Battle of the Crater, First Lieutenant Frederick Schneider (left) of the Second Michigan Infantry sat in a Confederate prison until February 1865. Lieutenant Colonel George Lockley (right) of the First Michigan Infantry was wounded at Hatcher's Run, Virginia, in February 1865.

There was General Philip H. Sheridan's cavalry raid against Richmond, in an attempt to destroy Lee's lines of communication and draw Confederate cavalry away from the main fighting. With Sheridan were the seasoned troopers of Custer's brigade. When the great Confederate cavalry leader General Jeb Stuart positioned his men in front of Sheridan at Yellow Tavern, about six miles north of Richmond, a brisk engagement developed on May 11, 1864. During the fight Private John A. Huff of the Fifth Michigan Cavalry got an enemy officer in his sights and pulled the trigger. Jeb Stuart, mortally wounded, fell from his horse. He died the next day. Less than a month later Huff also was fatally shot.

Grant fought on to Cold Harbor, where the Confederates had thrown up strong breastworks and lay waiting for an attack. When

Grant ordered a direct assault, his soldiers, sure of the fate that awaited them, wrote their names and addresses on slips of paper and pinned them on their coats so that their dead bodies could be identified. The Federal charge brought on the bloodiest moments of the war. In less than ten minutes a deadly enfilading fire accounted for most of the 7,000 Union soldiers that were killed, wounded or missing on June 3, 1864. The campaign was costly for both sides, but Grant stated in his official report that these battles, "bloody and terrible as they were on our side, were more damaging to the enemy."

After Cold Harbor the Union army crossed the James River and attacked Petersburg, Virginia, in an effort to capture the Confederate capital from the rear. Lee, caught by surprise, rushed his army to meet the threat, arriving in time to help General Beauregard repulse the invaders. Realizing the futility of assailing the Confederate entrenchments in front of Petersburg and Richmond, Grant settled down to a siege.

It was during this siege that the Federals attempted to break the enemy line by blowing up part of it, then attacking through the breach. Union soldiers dug a tunnel that extended from their position to a point directly below the Confederate works. Early on the morning of

On April 3, 1865, following a nine-month siege, the men of the Second Michigan Infantry (above) were among the first Union troops to enter Petersburg, Virginia.

Late-war heroes from Michigan included Captain John C. Hardy (left) of the Second Michigan Infantry, who played a prominent role in the capture of Confederate Fort Stedman, Virginia, and Colonel Benjamin D. Pritchard (right), whose Fourth Michigan Cavalry captured Confederate president Jefferson Davis in Georgia.

July 30, 1864, four tons of powder were exploded, hurling earth, guns, carriages, timbers and men into the air and left a 170-foot-long, 60-foot-wide and 30-foot-deep crater. After the explosion, soldiers from General Burnside's Ninth Corps belatedly advanced, the First Division in front, followed by Willcox's Third Division, which included six regiments of Michigan infantry. Federal troops poured into the crater until it teemed with humanity. Some of the Michigan men, unable to get into the crater, were hit by enemy troops entrenched on either side. By then, Willcox reported:

> *The enemy had recovered from their surprise, and now concentrated so heavy a fire upon the point that our troops, in seeking temporary shelter, became still more mixed with each other and with the First Division, and lost their ranks and much of their regimental organization, in spite of the efforts of many of the officers, and every new regiment that marched into the breach only increased the huddle and confusion, and interferred with the officers in reforming for another advance.*

As Confederate artillery slaughtered scores of men in the crater, the Federals found the hole so deep that it was difficult to get to the rim and fire back. Confederate infantry rushed to meet the threat; some advanced to the very edge and emptied their muskets into the sea of blue uniforms that carpeted the pit. Shortly after noon the brigade commanders ordered a retreat and the crater was evacuated. This operation, which cost Michigan 250 of the 3,800 Union casualties, was as Grant later commented, "a stupendous failure."

On April 2, 1865, Lee was forced to abandon Richmond. He headed west, hoping to join the Confederate army that was retreating northward in front of Sherman. Instead, the Union army surrounded him at Appomattox, Virginia, where, rather than subject his half-starved men to a useless blood bath, he surrendered to Grant on April 9.

All Confederate resistance ended that May—the month in which the Fourth Michigan Cavalry climaxed a fabulous career in a blaze of glory. The Fourth had left Michigan in September 1862 under the command of Colonel Robert H. G. Minty, an experienced cavalryman. Toward the close of the year, he was given a brigade in the Army of the Cumberland. Consisting of four cavalry regiments, including the Fourth Michigan, it soon became known as Minty's Brigade.

When Lee surrendered at Appomattox, the Fourth Michigan Cavalry, with Colonel Benjamin D. Pritchard commanding, was campaigning in the Deep South, where it helped capture Selma, Alabama, and Macon, Georgia. In Macon, word came that Jefferson Davis had fled Richmond and was believed to be in south-central Georgia. Davis had hoped to reach the trans-Mississippi, where he proposed to re-establish the Confederacy.

On May 7, 1865, Pritchard received orders to search for the fleeing president of the Southern Confederacy. At about one o'clock on the morning of May 10 Pritchard entered Irwinsville, Georgia, and learned enough from the inhabitants of the town to convince him that Davis and his party were camped about a mile and a half away. Before dawn the colonel and a detail of Michigan cavalrymen surrounded the encampment, surprising and capturing every one of the occupants. In

While Michigan mourned the death of Abraham Lincoln at a memorial service in Detroit (above), the Twenty-fourth Michigan served as the honor guard at the slain president's funeral in Spring-field, Illinois. At left are members of that regiment. Augustus Pomeroy, seated on the right, is the only identified soldier in this image.

accordance with orders from Washington, Pritchard delivered Davis to Federal authorities at Fortress Monroe in Virginia.

Meanwhile, in the midst of rejoicing over the end of the Civil War, the people of the land were shocked and saddened by the death of Lincoln. A Michigan private wrote that the soldiers in his regiment "appear as if their best friend had been assassinated." Another Michigan soldier remembered how joyful the men were that peace had been declared. But, he added, the men "felt verry sad . . . when ower Connel

called us out and red the order to us of the death of that Good Old Man the President of the United States. Then it was that you could have seen strong men shed tears of grief."

Lincoln, like those who fell on the battlefields, was a casualty of the war and the men in uniform knew it.

During the four years of conflict, over 90,000 Michigan men—85,000 of them volunteers—answered the call to arms. Not all of them saw action; some never left the state. Many were decorated or cited for valor; 67 were awarded the congressional Medal of Honor. In this titanic struggle—the nation's bloodiest war—about 14,000 Michigan men lost their lives. Over 4,100 were killed or mortally wounded in battle, about 10,000 died from disease. Those who survived the war returned home, most to live in relative obscurity. But until their dying day they never forgot the years they wore the Union blue. Nor should we forget. For they fought, as Lincoln said, to determine whether a democracy, here or elsewhere, could long endure.

Mindful of what Michigan soldiers did to advance the democratic ideal, it is appropriate to recall the words of a brigade leader who saluted his command for a splendid performance in battle: "Soldiers, your country thanks you, and will remember you in history."

Michigan Civil War Centennial Observance Commission

• • • • • • •

As the one hundredth anniversary of the American Civil War approached, the nation prepared to celebrate. President John F. Kennedy appointed Civil War historian James I. Robertson Jr. to chair the national committee overseeing commemoration activities. One of Robertson's first acts was to ensure involvement in the Civil War centennial by all the states.

Michigan began preparing for the centennial in 1958, when Governor G. Mennen Williams appointed the 26-member Governor's Civil War Centennial Commission that August. However, the commission's size, lack of funding and negligible clerical support kept it from reaching its goals. The following year Governor Williams signed House Bill No. 220, creating the nine-member Michigan Civil War Centennial Observance Commission. Scheduled to take effect on March 19, 1960, the following members were appointed: Floyd L. Haight (chairman), Richard Sonderegger (vice chairman), W. E. C. Huthwaite (secretary), James M. Babcock, F. Clever Bald, Robert J. McIntosh, George A. Osborn, Frederick D. Williams and Beulah Whitby.

The commission did not want to "celebrate" the Civil War, preferring instead to "commemorate and preserve the ideals, heroism and sacrifice of our Michigan forebears." The commission urged local Civil War observance chapters to seek, collect and save valuable war diaries, letters, pictures, newspaper articles and other memorabilia so that important Civil War events and activities related to Michigan could be preserved.

Instead of focusing on the overdramatized, often-published accounts of battles, generals and campaigns, the commission actively studied and illustrated how the Civil War affected and influenced Michigan's citizens (civilians and soldiers), resources and culture. Thirty committees researched, compiled and prepared previously unpublished materials concerning the Civil War's impact on Michigan women, African Americans, education, mining, labor, manufacturing, religion, farming, music, law and newspapers. Other committees studied Michigan's Civil War regiments, grave registrations, monuments, seals and emblems, battlefield commemorations, museum exhibits, Medal of Honor winners, the Grand Army of the Republic and Civil War flag preservation. Eventually, the committees published over two dozen books and brochures concerning Michigan's role in the Civil War.

The commission dedicated Civil War markers and monuments in Michigan and at several national battlefields. The first marker commemorated the First Michigan Infantry's departure from Detroit in 1861. The centennial commission also placed a state marker to honor the Michigan men who fought at Stones River in Murfreesboro, Tennessee, from December 31, 1862, to January 2, 1863. On July 1, 1966, members of the centennial commission, the Michigan Historical Commission and the Historical Division of the Michigan Department of State (now the Michigan Historical Center) participated in ceremonies at Stones River National Battlefield that honored the Michigan units who fought there—the Twenty-first, the Eleventh and the Thirteenth Michigan Infantries; the Fourth Michigan Cavalry; the First Michigan Engineers and Mechanics; and Battery A, First Michigan Light Artillery.

The commission's third major project was preserving Michigan's Civil War flags. In 1960 the Flag Preservation Committee's report listed 157 Michigan flags and guidons from the Civil War. Restoration costs were estimated at $13,500; the Michigan legislature enthusiastically approved an appropriations bill for the funds. The bill, which included a transfer of authority for the flags from the Department of Administration to the Michigan Historical Commission, was signed on May 23, 1963, by Governor George B. Romney. Flags from the first sealed case were removed on September 10 and sent to flag preservation specialists in New York. Less than a year later the flags were returned and then rededicated on May 22, 1964, by the commission.

After six years of service, the Michigan Civil War Centennial Observance Commission disbanded on June 30, 1966. Overwhelming public response and praise for the centennial commission programs and activities showed that it successfully commemorated a truly remarkable, historic American event.

Michigan's Out-of-State Civil War Markers and Monuments

• • • • • • •

D uring the late nineteenth and early twentieth centuries Michigan Civil War veterans dedicated monuments to Michigan units at the **Chickamauga and Chattanooga National Military Park**, Fort Oglethorpe, Georgia; the **Gettysburg National Military Park**, Gettysburg, Pennsylvania; the **Shiloh National Military Park**, Shiloh, Tennessee; the **Vicksburg National Military Park**, Vicksburg, Mississippi; and the **Andersonville Prison**, Andersonville, Georgia.

The accomplishments of Michiganians are recognized with state markers at the **Perryville Battlefield State Park**, Perryville, Kentucky; the **Stones River National Battlefield**, Murfreesboro, Tennessee; **South Mountain**, Braddock Heights, Maryland; and **Tebbs Bend**, Taylor County, Kentucky.

Michigan's most recent Civil War monument was dedicated in 1997 by reenactors of the Seventeenth Michigan Infantry at **Spotsylvania National Military Park**, Fredericksburg, Virginia.

The First Michigan Infantry fought in most of the Civil War's major battles in the Eastern Theater, including Gettysburg. Fifty years after the war's greatest battle, veterans of the First gathered on that same field to dedicate a monument recognizing the sacrifices of their comrades

Save the Flags

· · · · · · ·

O n July 2, 1991, Civil War reenactors from all over Michigan gathered at the state capitol. They were there to honor another celebration, held in Detroit 125 years earlier, when surviving members of Michigan's Civil War regiments entrusted the state with the battle-torn flags they had carried and cherished throughout the war.

More important, they came to help launch a project to save these flags—again. The Save the Flags program is dedicated to preserving the state's historic battle flags, properly displaying them and their histories with the public.

Preserving battle flags is expensive. One of the most meaningful and productive ways to raise needed funds has been through individuals, groups, families, businesses and communities that have "adopted" flags in the collection—to date over sixty-five. For more information, contact Save the Flags, Michigan State Capitol, P.O. Box 30014, Lansing, MI 48909, 517-373-5527.

Trace Your Michigan Civil War Ancestor

· · · · · · ·

S everal sources dealing with Michigan individuals and units are available and are valuable in searching for your Civil War ancestor. Most local and all county libraries have county history books containing lists of all soldiers and their regiments from that particular county. Most important is the 48-volume Michigan Adjutant Generals' *Record of Service of Michigan Volunteers in the Civil War 1861-1865* (also referred to as the Brown Books because of their brown covers). These volumes contain the military biographies of every Michigan soldier, sailor and officer. The volumes are indexed by the soldier's last name. *Michigan in the War*, an 1881 publication, contains a concise history of every Michigan regiment and battery; it also contains a biographical listing of all Michigan officers.

Suggested Reading

· · · · · · ·

There are thousands of books available on almost every aspect of the Civil War. To find out what books exist on particular Civil War topics consult *The Civil War in Books* by David J. Eicher, which gives an annotated bibliography of most Civil War books. For general understanding of military developments, strategies and events turn to James M. McPherson's *Battle Cry of Freedom: The Civil War Era* or *Ordeal by Fire: The Civil War and Reconstruction* or Shelby Foote's *The Civil War* (three volumes). Both of these authors give a well-researched overview of Civil War events.

Despite the abundance of books on the Civil War, there are relatively few books about Michigan's role in the conflict. Most regimental histories and accounts were written in the late nineteenth century by aging veterans. In recent years renewed interest in Michigan's Civil War history has brought many new books to the shelve. The most current book, Raymond Herek's *These Men Have Seen Hard Service*, chronicles the travels of the First Michigan Sharpshooters. Below is a list of the varied publications of the Michigan Civil War Centennial Observance Commission followed by a select list of other published accounts dealing specifically with Michigan in the war.

Publications of the Michigan Civil War Centennial Observance Commission

· · · · · · ·

Blum, Albert A. and Dan Georgakas. *Michigan Labor and the Civil War*

Cole, Maurice F. *The Impact of the Civil War on the Presbyterian Church in Michigan*

Day, Judson Leroy, II. *The Baptists of Michigan and the Civil War*

Dunbar, Willis F., ed. *Michigan Institutions of Higher Education in the Civil War*

Ellis, Helen H. *Michigan in the Civil War: A Guide to the Materials in Detroit Newspapers, 1861-1865*

Hawthorne, Frank M. *The Episcopal Church in Michigan during the Civil War*

Hayes, Frederick H. *Michigan Catholicism in the Era of the Civil War*

Hayner, Irene C., ed. *Materials on the Civil War Recommended for Use in Schools*

Lemmer, Victor. *The Impact of the Civil War upon Mining*

MacMillan, Margaret B. *The Methodist Episcopal Church in Michigan during the Civil War*

Marks, Joseph J., ed. *Effects of the Civil War on Farming in Michigan*

May, George S. *Michigan and the Civil War Years, 1860-1866 - A Wartime Chronicle*

May, George S. *Michigan Civil War Monuments*

McCune, Julia, ed. *Mary Austin Wallace: Her Diary*

McRae, Norman. *The Impact of the Civil War upon the Negro*

Metcalf, Kenneth and Lewis Beeson. *The Effect of the Civil War upon Manufacturing*

Millbrook, Minnie D. *Michigan Women in the Civil War*

Millbrook, Minnie D. *Michigan Medal of Honor Winners in the Civil War*

Millbrook, Minnie D. *Twice Told Tales of the Civil War*

Report to the Governor and the People of Michigan

Sexton, Evelyn. *The Impact of the Civil War upon the Congregational Church*

Teal, Mary D. and Lawrence W. Brown. *The Effect of the Civil War on Music in Michigan*

Wichers, Wynard. *The Dutch Churches in Michigan during the Civil War*

Wiegand, Roger. *Small Arms Used by Michigan Regiments in the Civil War*

Yzenbaard, John. *The Tri-State Soldiers' and Sailors' Encampment*

Select Regimental Histories, Diaries and Letters

. . . .

Anderson, William. *They Died to Make Men Free: The Nineteenth Michigan Infantry*

Bennett, Charles W. *The Ninth Michigan Infantry*

Benson, Richard H., ed. *Civil War Diary of Charles E. Benson, Seventh Michigan Infantry*

Bunker, Ren. *With the Western Sharpshooters: Company D, 66th Illinois*

Campbell, Alcetta G., ed. *Civil War Letters of Colonel Henry C. Gilbert, Nineteenth Michigan Infantry*

Crotty, Daniel G. *Four Years Campaigning with the Army of the Potomac: Third Michigan Volunteer Infantry*

Curtis, Orson B. *History of the 24th Michigan of the Iron Brigade*

Cutheon, Byron M. *Story of the 20th Michigan*

Ely, Ralph. *Diary of Ralph Ely, Eighth Michigan Infantry*

Genco, James G., ed. *Sound of Musketry and Tap of Drum: Letters of Harold J. Bartlett, Battery D, 1st Michigan Light Artillery*

Herek, Raymond. *These Men Have Seen Hard Service*

Kidd, James. *Personal Recollections of a Cavalryman with Custer's Michigan Cavalry Brigade*

Lee, William O. *7th Regiment Michigan Volunteer Cavalry*

Longacre, Edward. *Custer and His Wolverines: The Michigan Cavalry Brigade*

Nolan, Alan T. *The Iron Brigade*

Quaife, Milo M., ed. *From the Cannon's Mouth: The Civil War Letters of Alpheus S. Williams*

Sears, Stephen W. *For Country Cause and Leader: The Civil War Diary of Charles B. Haydon*

Smith, Donald. *24th Michigan of the Iron Brigade*

Sword, Wiley. *Sharpshooters: First and Second United States Sharpshooters*

Thornton, Leland W. *When Gallantry was Commonplace, Eleventh Michigan Infantry*

Illustration Credits

• • • • • • •

The photos and illustrations used in this publication have come from a variety of sources. *Michigan History Magazine* wishes to extend special thanks to all who contributed to this publication. The abbreviated credits are defined below:

State Archives (State Archives of Michigan, Lansing)
Grand Rapids (Grand Rapids Public Library, Grand Rapids)
Berrien (Berrien County Historical Commission, Berrien Springs)
Bentley (Bentley Historical Library, Michigan Historical Collections, University of Michigan, Ann Arbor)
Bozich (Stanley Bozich, Michigan's Own Military and Space Museum, Frankenmuth)
Broene (David Broene, Grand Rapids)
Custer Battlefield (Custer Battlefield National Monument)
Curtis (O.M. Curtis, *Twenty-fourth Michigan of the Iron Brigade*)
Finney (David Finney, Howell)
Western (Archives and Regional History Collections, Western Michigan University, Kalamazoo)
Livonia (Livonia Historical Commission, Livonia)
Library of Congress (Library of Congress, Washington DC)
Monroe (Monroe County Historical Commission, Monroe)
McGeehan (Albert McGeehan, Holland)
Mehney (Paul D. Mehney, Grand Ledge)
Michigan State (Michigan State University Archives and Historical Collections, East Lansing)
Record (*Record of the Second Michigan Infantry in the Civil War*, vol. II)
Reed (Patrick Reed, Lansing)
Rosentreter (Roger L. Rosentreter, Okemos)
Sickles (John Sickles, Merrillville, IN)

CREDITS: Cover: Duaine Brenner, reenactors: Paul Mehney and Josh Kuchmuck; p. 6, State Archives; p. 8, State Archives; p. 9, State Archives; p. 10, State Archives; p. 11, Bentley (left) Berrien (right); p. 13 Reed; p. 14, State Archives; p. 15, State Archives; p. 17, State Archives; p. 19, Finney; p. 20, Reed; p. 22, Rosentreter; p. 26, Mehney; p. 28, State Archives; p. 29, Finney; p. 30, Finney; pg. 31, Finney; p. 33, McGeehen; p. 34, Mehney; p. 35, Sickles; p. 36 Broene; p. 37, Finney; p. 38, Mehney; p. 39, Finney; p. 40, Finney; p. 41, Bentley (top), State Archives (bottom); p. 42, Grand Rapids (top), State Archives (bottom); p. 43, Bentley; p. 44-45, National Archives (left), Western (right); p. 46, Finney; p. 47, clockwise from upper left: Bentley, Custer Battlefield, Bozich, State Archives; p. 48, State Archives; p. 49, State Archives; p. 50, clockwise from upper left: Western, Finney, Michigan State; p. 51 Broene; p. 52, State Archives; p. 53, Bentley; p. 54, Grand Rapids; p. 58, Curtis (top), Finney (bottom); p. 62, State Archives; p. 65, State Archives; p. 66 State Archives; p. 68, Mehney; p. 70, State Archives; p. 72, Library of Congress (top), Finney (bottom); p. 74, State Archives; p. 75, State Archives; p.76, Record (left), State Archives (right); p. 78, State Archives (top), Finney (bottom); p. 82, State Archives, Back Cover: Rosentreter, Civil War monument in Stockbridge, MI.

About the Author

· · · · · ·

Frederick D. Williams is a distinguished professor emeritus and chair of the Department of History at Michigan State University. For nearly three decades, his Civil War course was one of MSU's most popular undergraduate offerings. Williams served on the Michigan Civil War Centennial Observance Commission and its publications committee. His long list of publications include editing *The Civil War Letters of James A. Garfield*. Williams lives in East Lansing with his wife, Florence.

Acknowledgments

· · · · · ·

Michigan Soldiers in the Civil War was produced by the staff of *Michigan History Magazine*: Dr. Roger L. Rosentreter, editor; Diana Paiz Engle, associate editor; Sharon E. McHaney, assistant editor; and Paul D. Mehney, editorial assistant. Text file production: Mary Jo Remensnyder, secretary. Order fulfillment: Joni Russell White, circulation clerk. Electronic production: Salt River Graphics/Shepherd.

Michigan History Magazine

· · · · · ·

Michigan History Magazine is one of the leading state history magazines in the nation. First published in 1917, the award-winning bimonthly offers a contemporary and colorful perspective on our Michigan heritage. Look for "Thank God for Michigan!," the 120-page Civil War collector's issue and *Michigan and the Civil War*, a select anthology of Civil War articles from more than 80 years of *Michigan History Magazine*. For order and subscription information telephone 1-800-366-3703.